Modern Love

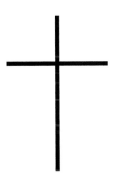

A Spiritual Journey

Other Books by Author

Forever Yours

Voices of the Past: A Small Collection of
Poetry

Modern Love

A Spiritual Journey

Andrew J. Ball

Lulu Publishing

Morrisville, New York

First Printing 2008

Library of Congress Control Number: 2008906225

ISBN 978-1-4357-2641

www.lulu.com

Lulu Enterprise
860 Aviation Parkway, Suite 300
Morrisville, NC 27560

Printed in the United States of America

Contents

My Journey

Deep Love

Love is a tree
Always growing.

Love is the sea
Abundant and eternal.

Love is forgiving
Pure, and untainted.

Love has no equal
And no rival.

Love is for everyone
Simple and true.

Wings of a Sister

You are the wings
That angel's use-

Love's wings
That people need-

Wings of the heart
That I know you have-

An angel on Earth
My beloved sister.

First Crush

I lived, but did not live
Looking at you from a far
But nothing more-
I wish, but dare not act.

I crave your attention,
Just one smile for yes-
Or head shake for no
Is it love?
Or something less- maybe more?

I like you! For now! And ever!
Be mine-
Make this sad, sorry man live
As if time elapsed.

Lonely Pain

Is there anyone who understands,
The pain that lurks within me?
Like a snake waiting in the grass.

Does God not hear me?
Does God not know,
What I feel everyday for five years now?
If only someone could understand.

Eye Opening

He who walks tall
With a smile warmer than the sun
And makes the rose seem common
Captures my fancy
Like a fly in a spider's web.

Does he see me the same?
Or understand how I feel?
If so (why then) does he remain silent?
Like the stars twinkling in the night
Standing in an endless sea of darkness.

He is the light
The light that shines on me,
Pulling me from out of the coldness
That froze me like a winter's frost
Unable to move or grow.

Looks are something,
But a kind heart goes a long way
Lasting more than a single lifetime
And giving hope to those like me
That their may be, someone who will love me.

To Emily-

We are the same
Elusive and unknown,
Only separated by time.

We both know that in the end
We are alone
And always will be-
It is our curse
That gives us freedom
To write,

We write from the heart
As well as the mind-
Thinking about death
And feeling what others feel,
Writing as we gaze
Through a window at the world.

As the Songbird Sings

Little bird, little bird
With gray feathers
And broad wings.

Little bird, little bird
Like a child's melody
Calming and peaceful.

Little bird, little bird
Why do you sit alone?
Why do you sing to me?

White Rose

It is the color of my soul
The purity of innocence,
Untouched- perfect as it is.
Nature's best creation
The rose of our everlasting heart,
Though appearing frail
It's stronger than stone
Withstanding age and time-
The Angel's gift,
Radiating God's never-ending love.

As the Blood Flows

The names are the blades
Cutting through my skin
And shattering the windows of my heart.

As the blood flows from my wrists
The poison seeps through my soul
Killing what little humanity I have left.

There is but one thought that runs through my mind:
In life I may have been hated
But in death I will be loved.

Though these images of suicide parade around,
Tempting my mind,
Promising a relies from the pain,
I stand strong in my pain
For as dark and gloomy as it may seem
The light will shine on me,
Bringing love in its wake
Whether now or in the distant future.

Beyond Tomorrow

The eyes shall see
What the mind knows
But the lips remain silent
Silent as the stars in heaven-
For what word of words can describe,
Or comprehend the meaning,
Of what the eyes have seen?

Voice remains still
As the mind races,
Knowing what has no form
That, which words cannot know,
This it is, for those who see beyond tomorrow.

Dream Guy

Is it so wrong?
To long for a kiss?
To feel your lips on mine?
O' how I dream of that.

You're the one I long for,
The only one I have ever wanted-
Yet I know that will never be
Pity- but my dreams will always be.

The Falcon's Travel

If my wings should touch the sky
My soul would fly,
Fly far and high
Beyond the winding river
Past the endless sea-

If my eyes should look out onto the horizon
My mind would wander,
Wander far and wide
Past the mountain's peak
Beyond the stars at night.

Dark Flame

Heart filled with sadness,
And a fire fueled by hate
Burning in my soul,
Bathing me in blood, flame, and rage.

God, forgive that which I cannot
Extinguish this dark flame
Let your undying love fill the gap
Give me strength, to stand tall.

High School Crush

Your tall sleek body
Plus the softness of your cheek
With the redness of your lips
And the soothing tone of your voice,
Plays on my affections
Just as the drummer would beat the drum.

I want you
More than the flower wants the sun to rise
Though I look away,
Just before you look my way.

I try to confide myself to the shadows of the room
So as to be left alone
Away from the others
Longing for you.

Would you have me,
As I would have you?
My body covered with disgust
And the unappealing weight-
Not as perfectly painted as yours
With the gorges black hair
And steely blue eyes.

Spirit Guide

I hardly ever see you,
Only in dreams
For my eyes are veiled
But I can feel you near me,
Calmness flowing from you.

My dearest friend,
Who was always there for me,
When I was a child
Playing games
And having in-depth conversations.

Your voice is powerful
Filled with encouragement,
Love,
Peace,
And guidance.

You're always there
Guiding me through life
And holding me close
With loving arms.

I'm not perfect
Making mistakes,
Yet your love is still strong
And you're never angry,
Distraught,
Or even disappointed

And for that I am grateful,
For you're the greatest
My dear friend and guide.

Blake

You are the light
That guides us all-

The light of love
That people long-

The light of the sea
That dazzles the soul.

Spare Friend

They treat me like a spare wheel
Not important
Only there for backup.

What did I ever do to you?
Care too much?
Ha, deceivers uncloaked!

I thought we were friends,
But blind I was to you-
No longer will your sharp jokes touch me
For your spell is broken,
I am free.

You renounce me
So I have forsaken you
Yet, in the name of love,
God forgive them!

Blind Mirror

I see it in the mirror
Staring back,
Looking repugnant.
Is it my own soul's reflection?
Or is it only skin deep?
It must just be flesh
For a few say beauty lives within,
But why can I not see it?
Is it my cures to be alone?
And be blind?

Abandon Cliff

Why did they abandon me?
Like the city in the cliff
I stand alone
Isolated from the rest.

Lust, for Another

Your eyes are like the sun and moon
So bright and luring
But beyond my grasp
And like a bat,
I am unseen and unheard.

Maybe one day you'll hear my song,
Calling to you if but for a moment
Like the songbird singing to its mate.

Christy

Can a rose smell any sweeter?
Or a candle burn any brighter?
It is your heart that sings the loudest,
Singing, singing, like the sea
Peace to those who know her power
Peace to those who know her love.

A child of the water
Swimming in the joy of life
Free of all earthly bonds
Free to love
Free to shine-
For who in the entire ocean shines the brightest?
If not thee?

A heart more precious than a pearl
More rare than any flower
More pure than rain.

Viper

She is a viscous viper!
Lurking among the shrubs
Waiting for the time to strike.

Fangs sharp as knifes
Filled with cold venom,
To kill her unsuspecting victim.

Shadow Heart

I find myself in shadows
Not knowing how
Or why I'm there.

I like the coolness of isolation
Yet desperately long for compassion,
The one human emotion that eats at me
Tearing me apart.

I hate it like a raging sun
Yet love it like a quiet spring.

The Day it Didn't Rain

The day it didn't rain,
Was the day hope was lost.

The day it didn't rain,
Was the day beauty died.

The day it didn't rain,
Was the day people cried.

The day it didn't rain,
Was the day I laid down and died.

Mary Springer

My tower of strength
Standing through the storm
Still beautiful in the rain-

My mighty mountain
Stronger
With every passing day.

My wise river
Winding through the land
Touching every life you come across.

My saint on Earth
Loving unconditionally,
No matter what we do.

Sensations

If I were blind
I could see with my ears-
See the sound
Playing my inner drum.

If I was deaf
I could see full color-
Color tempting my eyes
Dazzling my soul.

If I became deaf and blind
I could see with my mind-
See people for what they are
Never be fooled by their intentions.

Wolf in a Friend's Skin

Wolf in wool,
You cunning beast
Luring good people blindly to your lair,
Dark Shepard!
Conniving devil!
Trickster of the land,
Kill me swiftly!
Spare the blood,
End the pain filled heart!

Daughter

I know her name
The one who comes to me,
In my dreams.

A child
More precious than life
Just as pure as love
Untouched by mortality.

Long silver hair
Fair skin
Soft brown eyes, that see the beauty,
That is the world.

She holds my hand
And smiles
As we walk.

Though she never speaks
She is the voice of truth
A truth that polls at my soul
That which I'll never have.

Standing in Darkness

If I stood in the light
Darkness could never touch me-
I would be noticed
And no longer lonely-
Friends would be possible
Perfection underway.

But I live in the shadows of my sorrows
Away from any light
Watching others live and grow,
While I stay frozen in a lightless state.

O' how I long for the light
To have it touch my soul
Warm it up and make it shine.

Yet every time a mergence occurs, it fails
Like a candle in the wind-
Am I so bad?
Am I so repugnant?
Am I so horrible,
That all others are repulsed by me?

If God could see me,
God would see the tears
Pouring from out my soul
But others do not see
Especially those who were once close.

No body understands the pain
The hurt that keeps me in darkness-
It is not imagined
As some have said
But a deep longing blocked by a wall
And no matter what I do
Or how hard I try,
It still towers over me.

It is my fate,
It is my curse
Will it ever end?
Will the wall tumble into the sea?
I can only pray.

My God

You are my legs
That keeps me tall.

You are my strength
That guides me through life.

You are my courage
That keeps me going.

You are the light
That comforts me,
When I am alone.

You stand by my side
Giving me hope
That no matter what I do,
I do it all for you, my God.

You are my tower
My ocean
My heart's protector-
No one knows me better
Or loves me as much
My glorious God,
For you, I live
For you, I learn
For you, I grow-
I suffer without pain
Knowing that you'll always be there

And love me regardless.

Dreaming Name

I see the name,
The name that comes in my dream
Followed by two blue birds
That sings the beauty that is your name,
For what is a name?
If not our cover?

Silly Heart

What is love,
If not desire?
My heart longs for the day
When you'll be mine to hold and cherish-
If only I had a moment to speak with you
And know more than your name.

Singing Truth

Can I freely be what I am?
Will the judgment ever stop?
Will the sun ever rise?
O' songbird, say it be true
That society no longer looks down upon me
That I am no longer a second class citizen.

Why do they hate me so?
Why do they fear me,
As the fish fears the shark?

Little songbird, say it be true
Hope you sing, be true at last
That I can love who I wish
And have it treated like the rest.

O' songbird, let it be true
Stereotypes die
And hypocrisy fades
As families unite.

Dear little songbird
Why was I born this way?
Will anyone ever treat me the same as you do?
Sing me praise
For my lasting strength
That never dies.

Lily of Desire

If my desire should ever grow
It would blossom into a lily,
With each petal white as snow
Living freely in a pond
Becoming the symbol of my love.

Dragon Spirit

Her eyes see into my soul
The longing to be known and loved
Berried beneath the hurt and pain
Unseen to closed hearts.

Her tail swishes around us
Keeping the unwanted out
Like a whip
Fast, sharp in the wind.

Her breath of fire surrounds me
Keeping both of us warm
And safe
All fear is burnt away.

Her wings wrap around me
Giving protection
Comfort to my mind
My great protector.

She stays with me when I am down
Or in need
Both in spirit and in body
My animal spirit, the other guide.

Poison Rose

Your words are like poison in a rose,
Deadly to the touch.

Beauty as a cover
Foul, tainted from within.

Friend, no longer
Leave me be, deceiving rose.

Devine Truth

O' God who loves me
And helps me in my need
Why do your children persecute me?
Why do they say my soul is filled with sin?
Isn't love just love,
Regardless of whom it is?
Can a flower be anything less than what it is?

O' God who loves me
Be my strength
And help me stand
In this patch of thorns-
Send your angels
To be my shield
So that my heart be unbroken
By the knives that fly all around me.

Outside

Rain makes my heart sing-
Washing away the sorrow
Purifying my body-
Rinsing my spirit clean,
Until there's no more pain.

They call me strange
For dancing in the rain
But I know I'm not-
Every drop slides down my face
Taking away the heartache.

Faceless Name

Though my hands are cold
My soul in pieces
My eyes bleed
And my heart warm,
I long for nothing
Say the sound of your name
That heavenly chime
The one sound that brings peace,
Hope,
And comfort
In dark times.

Mary, the Saint

Mary be the name that angel's sing
While the harps chime in harmony
The harmony that is her name.

Saints look to Mary as their' own
One of the last saints on Earth
That loves everyone
Regardless of what they do.

People look to Mary as a queen
For no one is more understanding
No one, more kind
Or caring, as Mary-
A powerful woman
With a will unmatched.

The miracle of the will
Undermined by healers
Understood by family
Respected by all others.

A legacy of more than five generations,
Always look to her
The wise and powerful elder
Though some are blind
And deaf to Mary's truth-
I hear her like a bell
Ringing, ringing in my ears
Tolling in the hour of prayer,

But who amongst the new generations listens?
Who looks upon the old with respect?
Who understands the teachings of Mary?
I do, even when others close their eyes and ears.

Why does love fail in a world of hate?
The truth is, it doesn't
People just turn away
Afraid to love
And be loved.

If there was one lessen that Mary teaches
It would be this:
Love is never wasted!
It comes back to us eventually
And touches others who need it most
For that is the nature of love,
To be as a river
And bring life to barren places
Before meeting the sea
And adding to its might
For love has no equal
And will never fail.

Mary, you teach us so much
That is why we sing your name
Bringing hope in our hour of need
Giving us peace when we're lonely-
It is her name that I sing
The name that Cherubs sing
The only name that makes the songbird sing.

Crowned Heart

My heart is my greatest treasure
Pure, like rain
Beautiful, like a red rose
All mine and mine alone.

At times I wear it like a crown
So that all others may see
Yet at other times,
I keep it in the dark
So that it's glory can only be seen by me.

No one has ever touched it
Or loved it as I do
Though I wish for the fable love
That can rightfully claim it
And love so as I do.

If I Was Deaf

If I was deaf
I could feel the words
And the music,
Every note ringing in me like a bell
Like a string humming with every stroke.

But I am not deaf
I hear every beat and note
But I still appreciate every sound
Like the whale in the sea.

Timid Heart

Why do I feel with a heart
Yet think with a mind?
I wish I could think no more-
It hurts too much to dwell on you.

You with your dazzling looks,
And perfect face, shaped by angels
That surround you wherever you go-
I long for you
More than anyone.
If only I were brave,
Then you would be mine-
But beauty cannot love ugly as I.

If love were attraction
You would have my heart.

Waiting Love

When will love come for me?
When will I be free,
To be loved and liked by another?
I wait like a bear for spring
Always hopeful
That the next day will be the day.

The years roll by
Like an endless blizzard
But my heart keeps me going
Keeping me warm
The hope that there will be,
Someone for me.

Until that glorious day
I bide my time
Waiting beneath the freezing snow
For that one warm day
That will melt the ice
And set me free.

9

N is for the notion of power
That nothing passes it
The last true number.

I is for invulnerability
For nothing can hurt it
And nothing can help it
For it is but a number.

N is for nexus
The mystical force
That surrounds its origins
Unknown to the rest.

E is for entropy
Order to disorder
Simple to complex
The nature of number nine.

I Hold it True

I hold it true,
To feel his lips on mine
The warmth of his lips
That strong breath so close,
I shudder with an ever lasting yearn-
If only he sees me the same
Wanting me the same,
Hoping he returns the feeling
Though I'll never know.

The Blooming Mother

With every breath the rose will take
Beauty shall reside in you,
For you are a rose-

Red petals of your heart
Layers upon layers of love
Given freely to all you touch,
For there is no creature in Heaven
Or on Earth
That is as rare a rose as you are.

No flower blooms as big as you
When you open your heart up
And love-
For that makes you the rarest of treasures
That resides in my utopia.

My Painful Heart

Heart of passion-
Heart of love-
Remember me
As I forget to love.

Heart I shall forget you-
A useless thing
That eats at me
From the inside.

If love was strong
Things would be better-
No more pain,
No more sorrow,
But for me, love is not strong
I wish I had no more feelings
Just the coldness of stone.

If love was real
I'd have someone-
God knows I've tried
Yet things remain the same-
Is it the people?
Or is it me?

Heart I shall forget you-
The maker of my pain,
The once bringer of joy
Lay forgotten in my soul

For I no longer need you anymore.

The Fern Tree

On the slopes of a grassy hill
The songbird sings its name
Bringing peace throughout the valley
Helping life touch the heavens
And rain, replenish the green.

But as people move in
And develop the land
The green is lost
And only death remains.

No longer does the songbird sing
No longer does life touch the sky
The city replaces the trees
And only dirty rain falls.

The once proud, ancient, fern tree, is no more
No longer standing on the grassy hill
Not even a stump remains.

The songbird sits upon a sky rise
Looking out at its once beautiful home
And sitting where its friend once grew
The songbird cries,
But no longer sings.

My Burden

The sea is my blanket
Comfort amongst the sadness
That is apart of my life,
Fallowing me wherever I go.

Loneliness,
The thing I live
Eats at me from within
Leaving me a hallow shell,
Like the seashells in the sea.

Try as I might
I can never escape it
Making friends who only disappear
Leaving me in the cold
Why do I suffer so,
Unlike anyone else?

People look at me as though an ugly shell
Unwanted like the rest
But don't they see the pearl inside of me?
Or was my mother lying when she told that to me?

It is my burden to bear
That no one can understand
With a greater purpose than any man
It is for my God,
I endure it.

Frozen Eyes

Can I help what I feel?
A handsome face,
The feeling of desire
Pulsates through me
Like blood in a vain.

Is it their masculinity?
Or their warm gentle eyes?
Yes it is physical
The body shaking in nerves
While the eyes stay frozen,
Glued to their face
Longing for, a moment's peace.

Little Songbird

Little songbird at my window seal
That sings me joyful songs
You are my only friend
For others walk away.

Is it my stern appearance?
Or can they not see my broken heart,
That screams at the window of my eyes?
I must be repulsive
Though I try to do good,
And talk to people,
They look the other way.

Desperation is not part of me
Nor what I feel
But maybe that is what they see
Though that is not what I am.

Perhaps it is my maturity
Superior to my generation
Only understood by the elders
That gives me comfort
In this dessert period.

Little songbird at my window seal
The only friend
That does not fly away
Thank you for being my hope.

Standing on the Inside

I don't like to feel this way
Trapped in a room that's closing in.

Fear is my own reflection
Staring back at me,
How did I let it get inside of me?
When I should have been
Should have known
That I'm not the same man as I was before.

Why does fear always find me?
Trap itself inside me
Why can't I get away?
Find a place where I belong?
Maybe one day I'll find a resolution
A way to liberate my own confusion
But until that day
I'll never say, that I never tried to hide away.

Looking back on my life
I never knew
Never thought
Not until I looked inside of me-
But by then
It was too late
For I was in a room
With the walls closing in.

He Touched Me Like No Other

He touched me like no other,
With hands so soft and smooth
And breath, fresh, like morning dew.

In his arms my pain did die
Replaced with a steady calm,
My heart beating slowly with his,
Beating as one.

A kiss of passion,
Freed my mind
No longer bound to guilt or shame
Or petty judgment from the world,
Melting, like ice, from the warmth of his embrace.

Peace, in my mind
Peace, in my heart
As I lay next to him, undisturbed.

Remembering Tomorrow

Remember tomorrow, before it leaves
All the joys regained
All the sorrows lost
Rivers live, with cool clean water,
Valleys lush and green
Remember tomorrow, before it dies.

Black Rose

Black rose- black rose-
The symbol of my mournful heart
Longing for a nameless face.

Black rose- black rose-
Will this pain stay buried,
In my hollow grave?

Black rose- black rose-
The last life in all of Eden
Give me praise, for my long lasting strength.

Lone Horse

I am the lone horse
Abandon by the herd-
Or moved on,
I do not know.

I am a proud, noble, modest stag
Looking for a companion in the world
To share my life, love, and hopes with.
Though I may never find that equal
I'll still be searching.

Love, from God

I hear it in the rain
Drop by drop
As it slides down my face,
Rinsing my soul clean-
Each drop is like the ringing of a bell
Calling me closer to God, with every toll.

Angels wrap me in their' wings
Every feather brushes the fear away
Holding me in their love-
My body naked in the white light,
Basking in the glory of God-
His love becomes my truth.

No more pain,
No more fear,
Only love and joy,
At last I am whole-
The dove upon my shoulder
Giving me peace
And strength.

Red Rose

A rose is like a child
Growing, aging, and blooming
The purifying smell of life like a warm summer's rain
Like sweet dew at dawn in Summit Hills.

The red rose blooms
High above the jungle vine
Sweet red petals like cinnamon
When the storm parts and rain stops.

A solitary rose
The color of my everlasting heart
Its deep red keeps love living
The red rose, living in the canopy.

Singing Name

I hear the name the songbird sings
While sitting at my window,
It is the name that keeps me still
A name that has but four letters
Making my blood flow faster
As I think of you.

My Loving God

You gave me wings to fly
I tore them off
And you gave them back to me.

I fell to the ground
You lifted me up,
So I could stand tall.

You love me,
More than I could love myself.

You stood by me all the way,
And forgave me for whatever I did.

You saw the good in me,
When I was blind.

You gave me strength,
When I was weak.

You are my light,
When I am in the dark.

Through it all
I can only say thank you,
For loving me!

Dearest Friend

You are like a rose,
Whose petals open with the slightest touch,
Greeting the morning dew with fresh breath,
Pure
Untainted, by the air.

Do you hear the birds?
They sing your name,
Like an Angel's chime!
Harmony to all who hear it,
Peace to me;
Knowing that our friendship will last,
Regardless of the distance between us.

Essence

I am the water in the river,
The light to your sun.

I am the moon,
That lights your way.

I am the color and the clouds,
To your sky.

I am the voice in the wind,
The vary air you breath.

I am the love,
That all hearts feel.

My Conclusion

For most of my teenage years I have struggled to not only find acceptance among others, but also to accept myself for who I am. It has taken me years, but I can now look myself in the mirror and say "I love you." It has not been an easy journey and nor will life ease up. This is true for anyone, but for members of the LGBT community, we not only have to fight for equal right, acceptance among peers and family, but also have to come to terms with ourselves. Everyone needs to be able to stand proud and look at yourself in the mirror and love who you are. If you can do that, then love from another will find you, for it always starts with you loving you. Always, no matter what, be true to yourself!

I have found that life is nothing more than a spiritual journey. A journey that we all take, even though at times we wish we hadn't. For every drop of joy there is an equal amount of sorrow. How we learn from our trials in life shapes who we are and adds another brick to the monument that we build, that when finished, will glorify our souls; acknowledging to us the fullness of our spirituality. Spirituality is wisdom in its purest form. To gain wisdom we have to experience the knowledge (the emotion that reflects the intellect).

Thus far my journey through life has taught me one crucial thing that has forever changed me: Love truly does conquer all. Through all the hardship I have seen, and endured, Love has always been the thing that breaks the ties that bind and is the cement that holds us true to ourselves. Whether you believe in God or not, Love truly is the light that guides us through life.

About the Author

Andrew J. Ball is attending Hawaii Pacific University.